presents

MYDIDAE

JACK THORNE

Mydidae premiered at the Soho Theatre, Upstairs
on 5 December 2012

MYDIDAE

JACK THORNE

CAST

MARIAN
Phoebe Waller-Bridge

DAVID
Keir Charles

CREATIVE TEAM

Director	**Vicky Jones**
Producer	**Francesca Moody**
Designer	**Amy Jane Cook**
Lighting Designer	**Jack Williams**
Composer & Sound Designer	**Isobel Waller-Bridge**
Stage Manager	**Charlotte McBrearty**
Production Manager	**Ben Brown**
Production Assistant	**Mirain Jones**
Production Photography	**Lucy Patrick Ward**
Image Design	**Ian Bruce**
PR	**Chloe Nelkin Consulting**
Video Trailer	**Dan Pick**

Jack Thorne (Writer)
Jack's award-winning plays include *The Physicists* (adapt. Donmar Warehouse, 2012); *Bunny* (Nabokov UK tour/NYC); *Red Car Blue Car* for *Where's My Seat?* (Bush); *Greenland* (co-written for the National Theatre); *2nd May 1997* (Bush/Nabokov); *Burying Your Brother in the Pavement* (National Theatre Connections); *Two Cigarettes* (Bush); *Stacy* (Tron/Arcola/Trafalgar Studios); *Fanny and Faggot* (Pleasance Edinburgh/Finborough/ Trafalgar Studios); *When You Cure Me* (Bush); *Paperhouse* (Flight 5065) and *Solids* (Paines Plough/Wild Lunch at the Young Vic). TV includes *The Fades* (BBC3); *This Is England '88* and *This is England '86* (with Shane Meadows, Warp Films/Channel 4); *Cast-Offs* (Eleven Film/Channel 4) and episodes of *Skins* and *Shameless*. Films include *The Scouting Book for Boys*, which premiered at the 2010 London Film Festival and won Jack the Best British Newcomer Award. Radio includes *People Snogging in Public Places* (winner of Best Drama at the Sony Radio Academy Awards 2010), *The Hunchback of Notre Dame* (winner of the Radio Award at Ability Media International Awards 2009), *Left at the Angel* and *When You Cure Me*. Jack is currently working on numerous TV and film projects and is under commission to the Royal Court Theatre, the National Theatre, and the Royal & Derngate, Northampton. Jack's stage version of *Let the Right One In*, based on the cult Swedish novel and screenplay by John Ajvide Lindquist, will be produced by the National Theatre of Scotland and Marla Rubin Productions Ltd in association with Dundee Rep Theatre, directed by John Tiffany in June 2013.

Phoebe Waller-Bridge (Marian)
Phoebe trained at RADA and is co-artistic director of DryWrite. Theatre includes: *Hay Fever* (Noël Coward Theatre, West End); *Tribes* (Royal Court); *Rope* (Almeida); *2nd May 1997*, *Like a Fishbone* and *66 Books* (Bush); *Roaring Trade* (Soho); *Crazy Love* (Paines Plough). Film includes: *Albert Nobbs*, *The Iron Lady*. TV includes: *London Irish*, *The Cafe*, *The Night Watch*, *How Not to Live Your Life*. Radio includes: *Vincent Price and the Horror of the English Blood Beast* and *Burns and the Bankers* (Radio 4); *Money* (Radio 3).

Keir Charles (David)
Keir trained at the Central School of Speech and Drama. Theatre includes: *Red Light Winter*, *In A Garden* (Theatre Royal Bath); *Kursk* (Young Vic/tour); *Grand Guignol* (Theatre Royal Plymouth); *The Tragedy of Thomas Hobbes*, *The Taming of the Shrew*, *The Merchant of Venice* (RSC); *Elling* (Bush/Trafalgar Studios); *Pool No Water* (Lyric Hammersmith); *On the Piste* (Birmingham Rep); *Incomplete and Random Acts of Kindness* (Royal Court); *Romeo and Juliet* (Liverpool Playhouse); *Eye Contact* (Riverside Studios); *Keepers* (Hampstead); *Cadillac Ranch* (Soho); *Sunday in the Park with George* (National Theatre); and the touring production of *Oliver*. TV includes: *Watson & Oliver*, *Kate and William*, *EastEnders*, *Doctors*, *Fear of Fanny*, *HG Wells – A Life In Picture*, *Our Hidden Lives*, *Green Wing*, *The Bill*, *Dirty War*, *Family Business*, *Holby City*, *Ed Stone Is Dead*, *Attachments*, *EastEnders*, *Dinotopia*, *Band of Brothers*, *Always Be Closing* and *Keke see Keke do*. Film includes: *Across the River*, *High Heels*, *Low Life* and *Love Actually*. Radio includes: *Pandemic* and *Intent to Supply* (Radio 4).

Vicky Jones (Director)
Vicky Jones is a freelance theatre director and Co-Artistic Director of DryWrite, with whom she has directed shows at the Bush Theatre (resident company 2010–2012), the Roundhouse, Hampstead Theatre, York Theatre Royal, Liverpool Everyman and Trafalgar Studios. Directing credits include: *The Tour Guide* by James Graham (The Playhouse, Edinburgh Festival); *Stealing Sweets and Punching People* by Phil Porter (Nu:Write, Croatia); *Treemonisha* by Scott Joplin (Southbank Centre/national tour); *The Freedom of the City* by Brian Friel (Finborough); *Shuffle* by Polly Stenham, Bola Agbaje and DC Jackson (Royal Court @ Latitude Festival); *Zoo* by Dawn King (Arcola); *A Bedroom* (Lyric Studio); *Saturday Night* (White Bear); *Banned: The History of Censorship* (National Theatre Platform). Original workshops include: *When You Cure Me* by Jack Thorne (Lyric Studio); *Colder Than Here* by Laura Wade (Royal Court). As Staff Director: *Coram Boy* and *Rafta, Rafta* (National Theatre). As Assistant Director: *Piano/Forte*, *I Remember the Royal Court*, *The One With The Oven*, *Rampage* (Royal Court); *See How They Run* (West End/national tour); *Journey's End* (West End); *Meeting Myself Coming Back* (Soho); *How Love is Spelt* (Off Broadway, Summer Play Festival, 42nd Street). Vicky worked for six years as a workshop leader for the Young Writers Programme at the Royal Court Theatre.

Francesca Moody (Producer)
Francesca is a freelance creative producer. She is also Resident Producer for Look Left Look Right, Resident Producer for Undeb Theatre and Associate Producer at SEArED Productions. Recent credits include: *JOE/BOY* (We Were Here/The Last Refuge); *You Once Said Yes* (Roundhouse/LIFT Festival/Manchester Lowry); *NOLA* (Underbelly /Escalator East to Edinburgh); *Not Another Musical*, *The Welsh Atlantis* (Latitude Festival); *Brimstone and Treacle* (Arcola); *Rose, The Ducks* (Pleasance); *Out of Love* (White Bear); *Teddy and Topsy* (Old Red Lion). Future projects include: *My Name is Rachel Corrie* (RT Productions/Sphinx/Mull Theatre); *Youth* by Brad Birch (Undeb Theatre). *Mydidae* is Francesca's first project with DryWrite.

Amy Jane Cook (Designer)
Amy Jane Cook trained at Motley Theatre Design School. Theatre credits include: *Where The Mangrove Grows* (Theatre503); *I Heart Peterborough* (Pleasance Edinburgh/Soho); *The 8th* (UK tour/Paines Plough); *Mudlarks* (Bush/HighTide Festival); *65 Miles*, *Once Upon a Time in Wigan* (Hull Truck/Paines Plough); *Hamlet* (Young Vic/Maria Theatre); *66 Books*, *Flooded Grave*, *Where's My Seat?* (Bush); *The Water Engine* (Old Vic Tunnels); *The Pride* (BeMe Theatre, Munich); *A Midsummer Night's Dream* (Broadway Theatre); *W11* (Gate); *She Stoops to Conquer* (Hoxton Hall); *It's About Time* (Nabokov/Latitude); *Love's Labour's Lost* (Guildford Castle); *Limehouse Nights* (Limehouse Town Hall); *Ignite* (Complicité/Artsdepot); *Manor* (Soho/Tristan Bates). Film credits include: *Fred's Meat* (as art director, North London Film Awards).

Jack Williams (Lighting Designer)
Jack is Head of Lighting at the Royal Court Theatre. As Designer: *Ding Dong the Wicked*, Re-Lighter – *Vera Vera Vera* (Royal Court); *Cowardy Custard, Les Misérables* (Canterbury Marlowe Theatre); *The Storm, The Killing Game* (Battersea Arts Centre); *Book of Little Things* (Ovalhouse). As Associate Designer: *Ragtime, A Midsummer's Night Dream* (Regent's Park). As Assistant Designer: *The Magic Flute, Albert Herring* (British Youth Opera). Production Lx/Re-Lighter: *Scrooge the Musical, Half a Sixpence* (UK tours); *Joseph and the Technicolor Dreamcoat* (Japan); Holland Park Opera, *La Cage aux Folles* (Playhouse); *Dreamboats and Petticoats* (Savoy/Playhouse/UK tour); *Swallows and Amazons* (Vaudeville); *Plague Over England* (Duchess); Pleasance 2007–2011 (Edinburgh).

Isobel Waller-Bridge (Composer & Sound Designer)
Theatre includes, as Composer and Sound Designer: *Gruesome Playground Injuries* (Gate); *Blink* (Traverse/Soho); *The Girl With The Iron Claws* (Soho); *Head/Heart* (Bristol Tobacco Factory). As Musical Director: *A Woman Killed with Kindness* (National Theatre); *A Christmas Carol* (Library, Manchester). As Music Associate, and musician: *The Children's Hour* (Comedy); *Rocket to the Moon, Welcome to Thebes* (National Theatre). Film, TV and radio includes, as Composer: *The Frozen Planet: Freeze Frames* (BBC); *Secret Symphony* (Samsung/ The Times); *Gilead* (Radio 3); *Physics* (Winner of LFC Best of Boroughs 2012 @ BFI); *Ellie, Disaffected, Beautiful Enough, Hometown, Meeting Mr Tiller* (all shorts). As Orchestrator/Arranger: *The Imposter* (Film4); *Life, Planet Earth Live!* (BBC); *The Bounty Hunter* (Columbia Pictures); *The Day of the Flowers* (dir. John Roberts); *Route Irish* (Sixteen Films).

Charlotte McBrearty (Stage Manager)
Trained at Arts Institute of Bournemouth. Recent theatre includes: *Dora Live* (Life Like Touring); The TS Elliot US/UK Exchange (Old Vic New Voices); *Not Another Musical* (Look Left, Look Right); *Epidemic* (Old Vic New Voices); *Brothers in Arms* (Green Shoot Productions); *Trouble in Tahiti/The Telephone* (Wexford Opera Festival); *Don Giovanni, La bohème* (OperaUpClose); *Winners* (Wexford Opera Festival); *Shrunk* (Good Night Out Presents); *A Model for Mankind* (Good Night Out Presents). TV includes: *Spy* (Hat Trick); *Rush Hour* (Zeppatron).

Ben Brown (Production Manager)
Trained at Central School of Speech and Drama. Theatre includes, as Production Manager: *Where The Mangrove Grows* (Theatre503); *Mudlarks* (Hightide/Bush); *Dance Umbrella, Dance United* (Platform Theatre); *20/20* (LIFT/Platform Theatre). As Assistant Production Manager: *Port* (National Theatre); *Wild Swans* (Young Vic).

Mirain Jones (Production Assistant)
Mirain graduated in Drama at the University of Exeter in 2011. She began 2012 by interning with Clod Ensemble and was a production assistant for BABEL (World Stages London), a BAC and WildWorks collaboration. Recently, she assisted Look Left Look Right with three productions within three months, including the award-winning *You Once Said Yes* (Roundhouse). She was also Production Assistant on the transfer of *You Once Said Yes* to The Nuffield, Southampton.

www.drywrite.com

DryWrite is a new-writing theatre company that challenges writers to work with specific briefs and goals to actively engage audiences with argument and action. Founded in 2007 by Co-Artistic Directors Vicky Jones and Phoebe Waller-Bridge, DryWrite has since worked with over one hundred playwrights. They have produced original work for theatres including the Roundhouse, York Theatre Royal, Hampstead Theatre, Trafalgar Studios, Latitude Festival and were Company in Residence for a year at the Bush Theatre.

Notes from the Artistic Directors

In 2007, early in our careers and having a shared a pretty awful experience with a pretty awful theatre company, we decided to make our own work with the people who inspire us the most. We were inexperienced but hungry for a genuinely creative environment and determined to create it.

We came up with the idea for anonymous writing nights. These grew into monthly one-off events with up to fifteen writers invited to write to briefs based on ideas we wanted to explore. For example:

I Can't Believe It's Not Verbatim Theatre
Is an authentic voice impossible to mimic?

Writers had the choice to submit a piece of verbatim theatre or try and fake it. The audience had to guess which were the authentic ones.

Deadlines were short. Writers wouldn't have much more than a week to complete their piece, actors were rehearsed on the day, the audience didn't know who had written what and we just hoped no one would fall down the hole in the floor of the upstairs storage room in The George Tavern.

The response was huge and we became increasingly ambitious about what we wanted to see tested on the stage. The briefs were becoming more specific:

Guilty
How do you get an audience to care about a character who has committed a heinous crime?

Writers are each given a headline detailing a terrible crime committed. They are challenged to write the criminal justifying their crime by giving the context. The audience votes Guilty or Not Guilty by moving to the designated side of the theatre.

The Mob
How you make an audience heckle?

Writers are given the challenge to galvanise the audience without them knowing.

Funny, Not Funny
How do you make an audience uncomfortable about the fact they are laughing?

Writers are asked to tread the line between what is funny and what is definitely *not*… funny.

Our ideas led us to combine new writing with fight directors at Latitude Festival, choreographers at the Roundhouse and dance/radio experiments at York Theatre Royal. We were lucky to work with extraordinary writers, directors, actors, choreographers, composers and dancers at all stages of their careers.

DryWrite endeavours to ask questions through theatre. We will continue to set writers challenges engaging our audience in debates and arguments about how we live today.

With an interest in exploring privacy and intimacy, we set Jack Thorne the challenge to write a full-length play about a man and a woman, set in their shared domestic bathroom.

Thank you for supporting us and we hope to see you at our next production.

Phoebe and Vicky
Artistic Directors

Thanks

DryWrite would like to thank the following people and organisations without whom this production would not have been possible:

Steve Marmion, Joe Murphy and all at the Soho Theatre, Mark Shepherdson, Rachel Tyson, the Bush Theatre, Jock Rutherford, Isobel Williams, Neil Jeffares, IdeasTap, everyone involved in the Good Clean Fun fundraising production, Tree Waller-Bridge and the rest of the Waller-Bridge family, the Joneses, Peter Moody, Nico Ward Jackson, Jess Harwood, Adam Brace, Tom Salinsky, Deborah Frances-White, Rachel Taylor, Rachel Mason, Stephen, Aileen and James at Hatton McEwan, Michael Shelford and everyone who contributed to our WeFund.

www.sohotheatre.com

London's most vibrant venue for new writing, comedy and cabaret.

Bang in the creative heart of London, Soho Theatre is a major new-writing theatre and a writers' development organisation of national significance. With a programme spanning theatre, comedy, cabaret and writers' events and home to a lively bar, Soho Theatre is one of the most vibrant venues on London's cultural scene.

Soho Theatre owns its own central London venue housing the intimate 150-seat Soho Theatre, our 90-seat Soho Upstairs and our new 1950s New York meets Berliner cabaret space, Soho Downstairs. Under the joint leadership of Soho's Artistic Director Steve Marmion and Executive Director Mark Godfrey, Soho Theatre now welcomes over 150,000 people a year.

> 'Soho Theatre was buzzing, and there were queues all over the building as audiences waited to go into one or other of the venue's spaces. I spend far too much time in half-empty theatres to be cross at the sight of an audience, particularly one that is so young, exuberant and clearly anticipating a good time.' Lyn Gardner, *Guardian*

Soho Theatre Bar

Soho Theatre Bar is a vibrant, fun bar where artists and performers can regularly be seen pint in hand enjoying the company of friends and fans. Open from 9.30 a.m. until 1 a.m., with free Wi-Fi, serving breakfast, lunch and dinner, with a new, super-quick and tasty burger, bagel, pizza and salad menu, Soho Theatre Bar is the perfect place to meet, eat and drink before and after our shows.

Soho Theatre Online

Giving you the latest information and previews of upcoming shows, Soho Theatre can be found on Facebook, Twitter and YouTube as well as at sohotheatre.com.

Hiring the Theatre

An ideal venue for a variety of events, we have a range of spaces available for hire in the heart of the West End. Meetings, conferences, parties, civil ceremonies, rehearsed readings and showcases with support from our professional theatre team to assist in your event's success. For more information, please see our website sohotheatre.com/hires or to hire space at Soho Theatre, email hires@sohotheatre.com and to book an event in Soho Theatre Bar, email sohotheatrebar@sohotheatre.com.

Soho Theatre is supported by Arts Council England and Westminster City Council.

MYDIDAE

Jack Thorne

For Sophie Gardiner

Characters

MARIAN
DAVID

ACT ONE

Scene One

MARIAN *enters the bathroom. She's wearing overlarge headphones.*

She's talking business French aloud. She's wearing knickers and a Minnie Mouse T-shirt. She's just slept in them.

MARIAN. Est-ce qu'il y a un service de bus pour aller à Paris?

Est-ce qu'il y a un service de bus pour aller à Paris?

Beat.

C'est bien le bus pour Versailles?

C'est bien le bus pour Versailles?

She picks up a toothbrush and begins brushing her teeth.

She continues saying French aloud.

C'est bien le train pour Lille?

C'est bien le train pour Lille?

She brushes her tongue.

DAVID *enters. He's on the phone. He's in a pair of grey boxer shorts.*

She stops talking. He doesn't acknowledge her.

DAVID. I'm going to start with that…

I'm going to start with that…

He looks at her. He makes a signal. She doesn't understand it and laughs. He frowns.

Because I want to open hard…

If I start with that…

Well. It's a matter of opening hard.

She washes the toothbrush and puts it away.

She turns off her iPod. She listens to his call.

She sits on the side of the bath.

She thinks and then takes out some dental floss.

She begins to floss. He looks at her as she does. He smiles.

She smiles back. She starts to sexily floss. It's a hard thing to do sexily. She laughs.

If we don't open hard…

It's not about what's right or what's – right.

He looks at her. He covers the phone.

I don't know why you floss after you brush your teeth.

MARIAN. I don't know either. Is he being a dick?

He goes back to his phone.

DAVID. It's my pitch. It's my pitch.

…

Yes. Of course it's our pitch. It's our pitch. But it's my pitch to lead.

He covers the phone.

Flossing creates shit in your mouth.

MARIAN. Ya-huh and I can taste it if I do it before.

DAVID. Taste what?

MARIAN. The shit.

He goes back to the phone.

DAVID. I'm the pitcher. That's all I mean by that. I'm the pitcher and… that makes me the leader.

I know I sound like a tosser.

I'm just getting words – mixed up.

No. I won't.

He covers the phone.

Still. It doesn't make logical sense.

MARIAN. You're talking to me?

DAVID. Yeah.

MARIAN. You don't make logical sense. He's being a dick, right?

DAVID *smiles. He talks into the phone.*

DAVID. Yeah... Yeah... Well, complain about it if you want to...

Kiss me.

MARIAN *laughs.*

MARIAN. You're talking to me?

He smiles. She does kiss him. With a smile. Gently. On the mouth. He breaks off and talks immediately into the phone. She frowns.

DAVID. Yeah. Yeah.

I know. I know.

MARIAN *thinks. She turns her iPod back on. She begins to recite French again.*

MARIAN. On est bien en direction d'Avignon?

On est bien en direction d'Avignon?

DAVID. I...

He exits. She looks after him. She stops. A thoughtful expression on her face. She looks in the mirror. She smiles. Then she doesn't.

MARIAN. On est bien en –

Then she exits.

Then DAVID *re-enters. Now off the phone.*

He begins to take a piss. It's a long piss.

He sings gently, 'If You're Happy and You Know It.'

He stops singing.

DAVID. I can't smell the asparagus.

MARIAN (*off*). What?

DAVID. The asparagus.

From last night.

I can't smell it.

Does that mean it was good or bad asparagus?

MARIAN *re-enters the bathroom.*

MARIAN. I don't know.

DAVID. Is it one of those things?

Apparently the more that beetroot reddens your piss, the better it is.

The best beetroot turns your piss to almost blood colour.

MARIAN. Is that right? What did he want?

DAVID. Stuff.

She starts the bath. She checks the temperature of the water.

He sings a little more. Just hmming it. Not emitting actual words.

He finishes. He shakes. He puts away.

MARIAN. It's taking longer and longer to heat up nowadays. Is that the boiler or the tap?

He washes his hands. She flushes the toilet.

I can't smell it either. The asparagus.

DAVID. No.

DAVID opens the bathroom cabinet and takes out some shaving foam and a razor.

MARIAN. So that's something…

DAVID *laughs.*

He lathers up.

He begins to wet-shave.

Men always look so stupid with shaving foam on their face.

DAVID. Do men?

MARIAN. What's wrong with that?

DAVID. How many men have you seen? Me. Your dad. Who else?

MARIAN. You resent my use of the plural?

DAVID. A bit.

MARIAN. Because it feels incorrect or because it makes me sound like a whore?

DAVID *takes some shaving foam from his face and carefully places it on* MARIAN's *nose. She lets him with a grin.*

DAVID. Suits you.

MARIAN. Thank you.

DAVID *squirts some more shaving foam and carefully applies it to* MARIAN's *arse. She lets him. With a grin. He squirts some direct onto her arse. She now has a bunny tail.*

DAVID. *Really* suits you.

MARIAN. Thank you.

DAVID *looks her up and down.*

DAVID. Are you putting on weight?

MARIAN. No.

DAVID. It's fine if you are. You're skinny as a thing.

I'm just interested.

MARIAN. No. I'm not.

DAVID. I'm just interested.

I think you are. You should get yourself weighed.

MARIAN. I do – I actually weigh myself.

I'm not putting on weight.

DAVID. I'm just interested. Like I say, it's not a... You're so thin.

A bit of weight...

MARIAN. I'm not.

DAVID *thinks and then doesn't push it.*

MARIAN *puts the plug in the bath. It begins to fill.*

DAVID. Paul wants to start with the gross output. Save the sales figures till the end. Leave on a high.

MARIAN. You want to start with the figures?

DAVID. Start with a bang. Work backwards from there.

MARIAN. I think I'd trust your judgement over Paul's.

DAVID. You are putting on weight.

Your arse.

It has more flesh on it.

Beat.

MARIAN. You're not exactly thin.

DAVID. You are thin. It's not a bad thing.

I'm just interested.

I like watching your body change.

Beat.

MARIAN. You're balding.

DAVID. I like watching your body change. Is it ass or arse?

MARIAN. I'm the same weight I always am. You're losing hair daily. Or at least monthly.

DAVID. Your body is reapportioning it then. Less on the arms.

More in the ass. The ass is definitely bigger. I like it. It's an age thing.

MARIAN (*sharp*). 'It's an age thing'?

DAVID. What? Yeah, I don't mean that like…

MARIAN. Full of compliments this morning, aren't you?

DAVID. I like your arse with a bit more flesh on it. I think it's arse not ass.

Before I met you, I was quite into fat girls actually.

MARIAN. You've told me before.

DAVID. Have I?

MARIAN. You had a theory, when you were drunk, that fat-girl vaginas were warmer than thin-girl vaginas. You asked me what I thought.

DAVID. What did you think?

MARIAN. It took me a while to make up my mind and then I tipped a Ribena over your pyjamas.

DAVID. Oh, that night.

MARIAN. Yeah. That night.

DAVID. Didn't we… after…

MARIAN. Yeah. We did. Ribena does funny things to a girl.

He smiles. She smiles. They're remembering something.

MARIAN *takes a towel from the rack and uses it to get the shaving foam off the back of her knickers.*

You were shaking in your sleep last night.

DAVID. Was I?

MARIAN. Shaking and grinding your teeth. Like a scared dog.

DAVID. Talking too?

MARIAN. No. No talking. Mum wants us to come by on Sunday.

DAVID. Yeah?

We're probably going to be busy that day.

MARIAN. I thought so.

DAVID. You're beautiful. You have a beautiful body. It's fantastic.

I'll never get tired of it.

MARIAN. Thanks for the forewarning.

DAVID. What? You're strange.

Beat.

MARIAN. Am I?

They slip into silence.

I know.

Pause.

I quite fancy a Ribena now.

DAVID *finishes wet-shaving. He washes his face in the dirty water.*

He looks at her carefully.

I had that dream again.

She sits on the toilet and pulls down her knickers.

DAVID. Did you?

MARIAN. With some slight variations. I was standing – naked –

DAVID. Obviously.

MARIAN. In front of this huge burning fire. In the middle of the countryside.

And my feet were buried in concrete.

And I had this desperate need – this overwhelming need – to begin to pee.

DAVID. Obviously.

She begins to pee. She laughs.

MARIAN. As if by magic...

DAVID. As if by magic...

MARIAN. Anyway, then I noticed these people – these grass people – these people made of grass – were watching me and were all masturbating – they can't have been more than three inches high but it was clear what they were doing – and I was – disgusted and started to shout at them all – and then you rode in on a small horse – to save me – and...

I was delighted and you started fighting the grass people but they totally overwhelmed you and slit your throat.

And so I was stuck there – for eternity – desperate to pee – naked – in front of these masturbating grass people.

DAVID. I had a dream too – I was being blown by a girl with really goofy teeth – like splaying-out-in-all-directions sort of teeth – like that guy from the Bash Street Kids.

MARIAN. I think it's weird that you don't remember your dreams.

DAVID. At least I don't have weird dreams.

Beat.

MARIAN. At least you don't.

DAVID. How small was my horse?

MARIAN. I don't know.

DAVID. Was it – I don't know – pygmy-sized?

MARIAN. You think it was a metaphor?

Because you were also murdered.

By three-inch masturbators.

DAVID. I don't know.

He sits on the edge of the bath.

She stands and then sits on his lap.

This isn't comfortable.

MARIAN. We just need to get through today…

Beat.

DAVID. I've got that pitch…

MARIAN. No. I mean…

DAVID. Yeah. I knew what you meant. I just meant it'll be harder for you because I've got my pitch.

MARIAN. Thanks for the concern.

DAVID. I'm not…

MARIAN. I know.

They sit for ages.

How big was my horse?

DAVID *just looks at her.*

Don't listen to Paul. Do your thing.

Whatever feels right in the room.

I don't know anyone better at sensing a room than you.

DAVID. Yeah. That is… Yeah.

Pause. He looks at her carefully.

Sometimes I really don't know what you're thinking…

MARIAN. Sometimes I don't know what you're thinking either.

DAVID. I'd like to – open your brain and climb inside.

MARIAN. Crack it like a nut.

DAVID. Crack it like a nut and then climb inside – to the soft gooey –

MARIAN. My brain isn't gooey – it's rubbery –

DAVID. To the soft rubbery inside…

MARIAN. And it smells vaguely of honey. My brain smells of honey.

DAVID. To the soft rubbery – honey-smelling insides beneath.

MARIAN *looks at* DAVID, *who looks back*.

MARIAN. No.

You wouldn't.

Beat.

DAVID. Yes. I would.

MARIAN. You've got such strong hands.

I like your hands.

It was probably a big horse.

Pause.

DAVID. Should I cancel the pitch? I didn't mean it'd be easier...

MARIAN. I know what you meant.

DAVID. I shouldn't be going in today, should I?

MARIAN. What do you think the masturbating grass people meant?

DAVID. Kiss me.

MARIAN. Okay.

MARIAN *does*.

DAVID. Kiss me again.

MARIAN. Okay.

They kiss again.

They begin to kiss more passionately. He rubs her arse, and then he reaches under it.

Really?

He begins to masturbate her.

Really?

DAVID. Yeah.

MARIAN. You're going to be late for your meeting...

DAVID. I've got time.

He kisses her again. She breaks off again.

MARIAN. You are.

DAVID. No.

It's the morning. I always cum quicker in the morning.

MARIAN. Romantic.

He kisses her again. He breaks off with a laugh.

DAVID. Masturbating grass people…

MARIAN. Says the man who always cums quicker in the morning.

He laughs and kisses her again.

ACT TWO

Scene One

The bath is still running. Music plays. Something simple and guitar-based.

MARIAN *is shaving her legs in a dressing gown with her legs in the bath.*

MARIAN. I am the Lord of Hellfire.

She bites her lip, thinking.

And I have come for your legs.

Her phone rings.

She looks at it.

She doesn't answer it.

She stands, half-shaved, and turns and looks at her (knickered) arse in the mirror, lifting her dressing gown to do so. She frowns. She stands on the edge of the bath to get a better look in the mirror. She frowns.

Mummy... what's a Lord of Hellfire?

She answers in a deep voice.

I – fucking – am.

She laughs. And then doesn't.

Scene Two

DAVID *is on the phone, he is now half-dressed, as he talks he stares at his hair. He brushes it forwards. No difference. He brushes it back. No difference.*

DAVID. We're a young company with an aggressive…

He opens the medicine cabinet.

No, no, that's fine…

He roots around at the back of it.

Well, we've had some concrete bites, if that makes sense, and actually we're going in today to…

He takes out some hair gel.

I could email you some thoughts… I can't keep… I'm late for my… I'm late so… yeah, I'd probably just…

And some contraceptive medication falls out with it.

He looks at it.

He looks again.

Great. Great. I'll do that.

He disconnects the call – he thinks.

He puts everything back in the cupboard.

Scene Three

MARIAN *stands on the scales and weighs herself.*

She looks at the scales. She stands off them.

She takes a breath. She holds her breath.

She stands on the scales.

She opens her mobile.

MARIAN. Hi, it's me…

Yeah. I'm in the bathroom…

Just standing on the bathroom scales…

Weighing myself…

To see how heavy I am…

I know I'm thin…

I know I'm thin…

No. I don't…

No. I won't…

Mum.

Yeah.

Are you in the mood for a…?

Yeah, so…

David's at work…

Yeah. I just want to go with someone…

I don't know…

Put down some flowers…

Yeah. Now?

I'll get the flowers...

Okay.

She disconnects her mobile.

She stands looking at the scales.

Scene Four

DAVID *is sitting (fully clothed in a suit) on the toilet. It's now evening.*

He has his head in his hands. He's talking on a hands-free.

DAVID. We're just out of a pitch and, uh... We've had a
number of bites and... well, angels and... well, more firm
offers and we're looking for specific... We do have a PDF
with some...

He takes off his tie.

Well, in the pitch just now actually the thing that excited
them was our... Great. Great. What's your email...

*He takes out a pen, he looks around for something to write
on – he begins to write on the toilet roll.*

Scene Five

DAVID *enters in a dressing gown and turns off the bath.*

He exits.

He enters again with tea lights.

He begins to light them. He places them throughout the room. What was a bathroom becomes a lair. Becomes a beautiful spot. Becomes somewhere with intensity to it.

A phone rings from off.

He listens to it.

DAVID. One alligator.

Two alligator.

Three alligator.

Four alligator.

It rings off.

He finishes lighting candles.

He looks around the room.

He exits.

He re-enters with some Febreze spray. He squirts it sort of artfully around the room. He smells the air. Then he smiles.

The fuck am I doing?

He thinks and then shuts the door.

He takes off his dressing gown. He's naked underneath.

He looks at himself in the mirror. He gives himself the appraising eye.

He turns around to look at his arse. He can't get a great angle in the mirror. He clenches his arse. He thinks. He clenches his arse again.

He turns back forward. He pushes his dick sideways. He does it again. He plays with his dick slightly so that it's bigger.

MARIAN *enters the room.*

I didn't hear you.

Beat.

MARIAN. I was quiet. I'm quite quiet.

What's this?

DAVID. It's for you. It's for us.

It's for you.

MARIAN. You're naked.

DAVID. I am.

Beat.

MARIAN. Why? Why are there candles here?

DAVID. For you.

MARIAN. You're naked – for me – and there are candles – also for me?

Beat.

DAVID. You're early.

I wasn't expecting you yet. I thought I'd hear you. This isn't exactly how I hoped this would go.

MARIAN. You really didn't hear me?

DAVID. No.

Pause.

MARIAN. Brought up by Indians.

DAVID. Yeah?

MARIAN. American Indians. I mean, quiet feet. Is that racist?

DAVID. Yeah.

Pause.

Hi.

MARIAN. Hi.

DAVID. You look nice. Your hair...

MARIAN. No.

DAVID. It looks different.

MARIAN. Are you leaving your dressing gown off?

DAVID. It looks different.

MARIAN. New shampoo.

I suspect.

Are you going to fuck me?

DAVID. No... Not...

MARIAN. Because as foreplay goes, nudity isn't especially subtle.

DAVID.... Unless you want to?

MARIAN. No.

And your penis is bigger than usual so that means you've been having some thoughts which are also not entirely subtle.

DAVID. No, I, uh, all I wanted to do is – I poured you a bath. I've got a... I've got... there is wine downstairs. Hold on.

MARIAN. Okay.

He exits.

She stands a moment.

Looking utterly lost.

She begins to cry.

He re-enters. She stops crying. He doesn't notice.

He picks up his gown and puts it on.

DAVID. Running through the house naked feels a little…

MARIAN. Flagrant.

DAVID. Exactly.

Entirely flagrant. Is that the right word?

MARIAN. Yes.

DAVID. White or red?

MARIAN. Red.

DAVID. Really?

MARIAN. Or white if you want white…

DAVID. Red's fine.

I'm just… red's fine.

DAVID *exits again.*

MARIAN *stands a moment again.*

She makes to decide whether she wants to cry or not.

She decides not.

Pause.

She makes a quick decision.

She takes off her clothes as rapidly as possible.

And then stands a moment, breathes, looks at herself in the mirror, and then climbs into the bath.

DAVID *re-enters, clutching a wine bottle, and two slightly oversized wine glasses.*

He's surprised to see her inside the bath.

You got in…

MARIAN. Yeah.

Beat.

DAVID. I was going to undress you.

Beat.

MARIAN. Were you?

Beat.

DAVID. I thought it might be nice…

Beat.

MARIAN. Like a mother and child.

Gently easing my clothes off of me.

Singing to me reassuring songs about farm equipment as you do.

DAVID *looks at her, not sure what she means, she looks back, not sure what she means either.*

DAVID. No, not that so much… more…

I don't know.

Farm equipment?

MARIAN. My mother had an odd idea of what was reassuring.

He looks at her.

DAVID. Wine?

MARIAN. Wein?

DAVID *smiles. He begins to open the bottle of wine.*

DAVID. Ja, wein?

MARIAN. Is it German?

DAVID. No. French.

She nods.

He pours her a glass.

In fact, madam… Now this, madam, is from our premiere range of French wines.

It cost a whole six pounds. Savour the tastes and smells. It smells like?

Yes. Tesco.

MARIAN. You're funny.

Beat. He's not.

DAVID. You're not laughing.

MARIAN. You're not that funny.

Beat.

DAVID. Room for a small one?

MARIAN. You're not that small.

DAVID. I'm smaller than you.

MARIAN. A lot of people are smaller than me. You didn't put enough bubbles in this bath.

DAVID. No.

MARIAN. I can't cover myself as much as I'd – like.

DAVID. You look great.

He takes his dressing gown off. He climbs into the bath.

It takes them a while to get comfortable.

If you put that there…

MARIAN. Like…

DAVID. Yeah.

MARIAN. Just move that…

DAVID. Yeah. Is that?

MARIAN. Yes, that's my vagina…

DAVID. So if I just…

MARIAN. Still my vagina…

DAVID. Hang on… I'll just…

MARIAN. Perfect.

They get comfortable. They're facing each other in the bath. He has his back to the taps.

He looks at her. She looks at him. She suddenly laughs.

DAVID. What?

MARIAN. Nothing.

DAVID. Okay.

But this bit deserves a laugh so…

She laughs again.

MARIAN. Sorry. It is quite…

DAVID. Why is that?

MARIAN. No, don't, it's lovely – jolly…

DAVID. Yeah.

MARIAN. Besides, I needed to laugh so…

DAVID. I was kind of looking forward to undressing you.

MARIAN. Were you?

DAVID. Yeah.

Pause. MARIAN *grins and starts singing the theme to* Record Breakers, *this is clearly a bit of a routine for them.*

She looks at DAVID, *she nods at him. He smiles – and then sings the next couple of lines with slight reluctance. They sing the last few lines together.*

They finish and both smile.

MARIAN. How was the presentation?

DAVID. They want us to come back with more figures. How was here?

MARIAN. More or less the same. The cat vomited.

So that was exciting.

I'm thinking of starting work again…

DAVID. Yeah?

Pause.

MARIAN. Only if you think…

Pause.

DAVID. Yeah.

Pause.

It's strange what you want permission for and what you don't.

MARIAN. Is it?

DAVID. Yeah.

MARIAN. What does that mean?

DAVID. I mean… I mostly mean, people generally, not – you…

MARIAN. Okay.

DAVID. This didn't start as I hoped.

MARIAN. No.

DAVID. I didn't expect you to find it funny.

Pause. MARIAN *thinks.*

MARIAN. What does 'more figures' mean?

DAVID. It means they need more information…

MARIAN. Everyone always needs more information.

DAVID. Yes. But they want more before they…

MARIAN. Fire the gun.

DAVID. And we couldn't exactly – we couldn't exactly demand an answer.

They know we're…

MARIAN. Weak.

DAVID. Exactly.

MARIAN. Not in a bad way.

DAVID. No. No. We've just got small… horses.

Pause.

MARIAN. You remember that time I got the squits in Zimbabwe?

DAVID. Not now I don't.

Now I'm choosing to forget such a moment.

MARIAN. No?

Okay. Just trying to be nostalgic… in the bath…

DAVID. We don't have the memories for nostalgia.

MARIAN. I know.

DAVID. Neither of us do. It's – we've never remembered anything…

MARIAN. And my nostalgia literally mostly relates to pooing and shitting. Which isn't really a nostalgia we can enjoy together considering your aversion to my pooing and shitting. I use both words. Why use one when two can do? Pooing and shitting. Now, that would be a great name for a band.

Pause.

First time you had your heart broken…

DAVID. What's wrong with just being a bit quiet?

MARIAN. Close your eyes. First time you felt like you were going to succeed at something, first time you can remember true fear, first time you felt intentional love for someone or something, first time you picked up an animal and realised you could kill it, first time you used the toilet in front of someone who wasn't helping you, first time you realised eating chocolate was bad, first time you had sexual feelings for a teacher, first time you had sexual feelings for someone you knew you shouldn't have sexual feelings for, first time you farted in a lift, first time you intentionally farted in a lift, first time you masturbated, first time you realised you weren't always going to have friends, first time you realised your friends weren't good enough, first time you felt genuine despair, first time you rode a bike without hands, first time you felt true shame, first time you pissed in a bath and meant it, first time you realised you were cleverer than other people, first time you realised you weren't as clever as you realised, first time you felt like your life had changed unutterably, first time you clearly remember lying, first time you remember giving someone something you didn't want to give, first time you had your heart broken…

You didn't close your eyes.

DAVID. No.

MARIAN. Pity.

DAVID. Yes.

MARIAN. Secondary school.

He was called Peter.

DAVID. Peter. I hate him already.

MARIAN. Because he was called Peter?

DAVID. Parents who name their kids Peter – it's generally, maybe subconsciously or… but it's generally after St Peter.

I think that's arrogant. Tell me more.

MARIAN. He was in a band.

DAVID. Drummer?

MARIAN. Drummer! Do I look like the sort of girl who'd date the drummer?

Guitarist.

Bass guitarist.

DAVID. Sexy.

MARIAN. Deadly sexy.

Brown eyes. Sculpted arms.

He had – what do you call that haircut that boys – he had curtains.

DAVID. Now I do hate him

MARIAN. Hair fascist.

DAVID. Yeah.

MARIAN. Wasn't Peter a shit saint? Denying Christ and…

DAVID. Only at that bit. And he needed to be. The rest of the time he was brilliant.

MARIAN. He called me 'his crumpet' – I think that was his attempt to be Cockney Gangster.

DAVID. Cockney Gangster?

MARIAN. I know, what did we know, we were at posh school, you were actually a – your granddad met Reggie Kray.

DAVID. Ronnie Kray.

MARIAN. Same difference.

DAVID. And he didn't 'meet' Ronnie, he stood up to Ronnie.

You were – you always get that story slightly wrong…

MARIAN. Were we talking about me?

DAVID. We were. You and the bass guitarist.

MARIAN *splashes* DAVID *with some water.*

MARIAN. Pour me some more wine.

Beat.

DAVID. Of course.

DAVID *does.*

MARIAN. This was nice of you.

To do the bath thing.

Sorry I laughed.

DAVID. Yeah?

Beat.

MARIAN. So the meeting was a write-off, a total write-off…

DAVID. Not a total write-off.

We've got another meeting.

MARIAN. Which will be your…

DAVID. Fourth.

They want projected international sales. They want breakdowns on parts.

They want to know assimilation costs and…

MARIAN. What did Paul…?

DAVID. 'We should have ended with the figures, if we'd ended with our figures they wouldn't have wanted more – figures.'

I don't want to talk about it.

You were telling me about Pete…

MARIAN. I was…

DAVID. Pistol Pete the bass guitarist.

MARIAN. I was.

DAVID. A man I love to hate.

MARIAN. He's now friends with me on Facebook.

DAVID. Is he married?

MARIAN. No.

DAVID. Is he fat?

MARIAN. No. Less hair though.

DAVID. Right.

MARIAN. Don't smile.

Pete and I first started going out on the biology field trip to Dartmoor.

DAVID. Dartmoor?

MARIAN. Was it biology?

May have been geography… Very interesting stones.

Stones.

I remember us having to look at stones. I don't know.

There wasn't even a gift shop so we were forced to spend all our money at a service station. He kissed me beside the fizzy-drinks fridge.

DAVID. Sounds romantic.

MARIAN. Very romantic.

I touched his hair.

He put his tongue in my mouth.

DAVID. Nice.

MARIAN. It was a tumultuous relationship.

Riven through with deceit, intrigue and band practice.

DAVID. I think I may be getting an erection.

Beat. She smiles.

MARIAN. We split up at Thomas Jenkins's house party.

DAVID. Thomas Jenkins's house party? Once again your school years sound like the Famous Five.

MARIAN. Thomas Jenkins was a cunt.

DAVID. Ah.

MARIAN. Did they have house parties in the Famous Five?

DAVID. No. But...

MARIAN. I thought they just ate ham sandwiches, drank ginger beer and didn't notice that girl having a gender crisis...

DAVID. George.

MARIAN. Now how did you remember that name – do you fancy her? You fancy fat girls and girls having a gender crisis.

DAVID. I never fancied George.

MARIAN. Thomas Jenkins tried to stick four fingers up my friend Shona.

She was in quite a lot of pain. She screamed. He didn't like her screaming.

Called her frigid and tight. There was some sort of play on words, her name and the word tight... Or...

DAVID. We hate Thomas Jenkins...

MARIAN. Slippery Shona.

Everyone called her Slippery Shona. To be fair, I may have called her Slippery Shona. The cricket team called her First Slip.

DAVID. Cricket team? Famous fucking Five.

MARIAN. You didn't have a cricket team?

DAVID. No.

MARIAN. Man of the people. Fucker of fat girls. I doff my hat.

DAVID. Thanks.

MARIAN. This wine is fine.

DAVID. Better than I thought it would be.

Beat.

MARIAN. Anyway – that night – Lizzie, year above, bit fat, terrible slut – you'd have loved her – gave Pistol Pete a blowie in Thomas Jenkins's garage beside Thomas Jenkins's dad's vintage Mazda.

DAVID. Can you – is there such a thing as a vintage Mazda?

MARIAN. Is that the point of my story?

DAVID. And you found them?

MARIAN. No… No… Not that kind of story…

No. He just told everyone.

Getting a blowjob was quite an achievement in those days…

DAVID. I can imagine.

Beat.

MARIAN. First heartbreak. I was fourteen.

I shagged Steve Bryson ten months later. Mainly to show I wasn't frigid like Shona and that I hated Pete.

DAVID. Fourteen?

MARIAN. I may have been fifteen by then.

We had sex in the public-school system too you know…

Pause.

You don't want to talk about it? At all?

DAVID. Pistol Pete?

MARIAN. The meeting.

DAVID. There's nothing to talk about…

MARIAN. But…

DAVID. I've basically told you everything.

MARIAN. I am in control of all the information.

DAVID. You are.

MARIAN. Go on then. First heartbreak.

DAVID. I'm not very good at this game...

MARIAN. All the same...

DAVID. Really? Can't we...

MARIAN. We can talk about your meeting or your first heartbreak. One or the other...

DAVID. I was considerably older.

MARIAN. That's okay.

DAVID. I was twenty. University.

MARIAN. This is all okay.

DAVID. Her name was Rachel Annes.

MARIAN. No, I already know about her.

DAVID. Well. She was...

MARIAN. The game is no fun if I already know about someone...

Beat.

DAVID. Well. That's what she was... She was my first heartbreak.

MARIAN. Yeah, well, there you go.

You were supposed to tell me something new.

That wasn't something new.

DAVID. You know me pretty well... No new information.

MARIAN. Did you know about Pete?

DAVID. Pistol Pete, the blowjob king?

No.

But you've had lots of boyfriends.

MARIAN. Well, yes, I have.

DAVID. Your information source is – wider – than mine.

I've had less girlfriends.

MARIAN. Yes. You have.

That's because you're sullen.

DAVID. 'Sullen'?

MARIAN. Girls don't go for sullen men.

DAVID. I wish I'd known that sooner…

Why are our conversations so inconsequential?

MARIAN. One thing I like about you is your ability to grenade-
bomb me with words more than two syllables. You don't do
it often. But I always appreciate it.

Pause.

DAVID. I thought I was quite full of life…

MARIAN. You're dynamic.

DAVID. I'll take dynamic.

MARIAN. And sullen.

Rachel Annes.

Two first names instead of one.

The girl was always cursed to fall in love with a sullen man
like you.

Pause.

DAVID. Yeah?

Beat.

MARIAN. Yeah.

Have you told me about all the fat girls?

Which ones were fat?

DAVID. Yeah yeah. Shit game really.

MARIAN. Only when I play it with you.

DAVID. I've told you about all of them. Fat and thin.

MARIAN. Okay.

DAVID. Shit game, you see…

MARIAN. Okay. So…

Okay.

Pause.

DAVID. Are you taking the pill?

Beat.

MARIAN. What?

DAVID. Are you taking birth control?

Talking of information.

Shall we talk about that…

MARIAN. Talk about what?

DAVID. Because I thought we agreed…

MARIAN. Thought we agreed what?

DAVID. That we were trying again…

MARIAN. When did we agree that…?

DAVID. We agreed that…

MARIAN. You agreed that.

DAVID. We did.

MARIAN. No. I still I was still – she was my – I didn't want a replacement just yet.

Pause.

Was that what this bath was about?

DAVID. Don't turn this…

MARIAN. Because I thought this bath was about you reaching out to me, we'd have an emotional bath, discuss things of inconsequence and go to bed and I'd sit on your face. But instead –

DAVID. I didn't want a replacement.

MARIAN. But instead this is an interrogation room, isn't it?

DAVID. I didn't want a replacement.

Beat. She looks up at his face.

MARIAN. Yes.

I'm taking…

Actually I am.

I'm taking. Yeah.

Beat.

DAVID. And you kept it from me?

MARIAN *looks at him.*

MARIAN. I didn't advertise it.

DAVID. You didn't mention it.

MARIAN. I just let you cum inside me under false pretences. Yes.

Sue my womb for flagrant lying. I apologise to all your unnecessary spermatozoa.

It's my body.

I didn't want to have an argument.

DAVID. So you let me hope?

MARIAN. I weigh the same. My arse isn't bigger.

DAVID. You let me hope?

I mean, of information that can be…

MARIAN. Looking at me all the time trying to work out when I'm going to deliver you version fucking two. Your much needed sequel.

DAVID. You let me hope. That was… that is… information I'd have…

MARIAN. My arse is exactly the same.

And don't even start to – don't even start to – when was the last time you went to her grave?

I had to go with my fucking mother.

DAVID. You let me hope.

MARIAN. No, I let you fuck me.

You did all the hoping by yourself.

Pause.

DAVID *makes to say something.*

And then says nothing.

DAVID. Okay. Here's something that you…

Pause.

Okay. Here's information…

Pause.

When I was at school – I got picked for my – can't have been more than twelve – got picked for my school's football team. Right-back.

It was a big moment for me.

Even bigger one for my dad. Because – um – because he was my dad and that's what they… He always said the reason why he didn't play football professionally was racism, he went for a few trials – he was shit.

The reason why he didn't play football professionally was – he was shit. But anyway, me being picked for my school football team. That mattered.

I was pretty shit too.

But I was willing and would run around a lot. And that's pretty much all you need to be a right-back.

MARIAN. I don't know much about football.

Beat.

DAVID. I know you don't. Anyway, I arranged to meet my friend Tony before the game. We said we were going to warm up together. He was making his debut too.

We went to the chip shop and bought a packet of chips which we shared. I remember it quite clearly. He put too much salt on the chips.

They tasted like shit.

Tony was a midfielder. Quite good. Sort of a midfield marauder but with a bit of elegance. Sort of Paul Ince-like.

MARIAN. I don't know much about football.

DAVID. Anyway, after about five minutes, these girls came over and started talking and, uh… We talked back. And then they left.

And then a couple of older lads with their own car – came over and gave us a couple of cigarettes…

MARIAN. You smoked?

DAVID. And then…

MARIAN. You always hate me smoking.

DAVID. And they said, we've heard about this thing – there's this old car up the rec and some kids are going to set fire to it you want to come watch?

We were due at school in about five minutes but Tony said 'yeah'. Immediately he said 'yeah'. And I said nothing. We drove up there. There wasn't anything on fire. The older boys said 'fuck it, that's annoying' and we said 'yeah'.

They didn't offer us a lift back. So we missed the football.

My dad asked afterwards whether I'd been ill. He was working nights at the time – couldn't get a better job – he took the night off to watch me play. I never made the team again.

Tony did.

Actually, Tony was eventually made captain.

You want to know when I first had my heart broke? Then. I was... I broke my own heart. That's what – that's what. I broke my own heart.

DAVID *sits for ages.*

DAVID *leans across. He touches* MARIAN*'s face.*

And then he thinks. And then he starts to push her down.

He starts to push her down. Under the water.

MARIAN. No... No... David... David...

He pushes her down under the water.

He holds her for what seems like too long.

He holds for what seems like way too long.

He holds her to the point where most would assume she's dead.

And then he stops.

And she re-emerges.

Breathing deeply.

And she makes to hurt him but realises he's not going to hurt her. And so doesn't.

And he looks at her. And she looks back.

And this lasts for fucking ever.

Right then.

They look at each other with deadly accuracy.

And then he stands up.

And he walks out of the bath and away.

Out of the room.

Dripping water as he goes.

Scene Six

MARIAN *gets out of the bath – she sits on the edge of the bath – lit only by candles. She sings something gently to herself. We don't hear what it is.*

Then she stands, picks up a towel and wraps it carefully around herself.

She leaves the bathroom.

Scene Seven

DAVID *enters, he looks around the room, he unplugs the bath, which begins to drain out.*

He looks at himself in the mirror.

He blows all the candles out.

He picks them up. He takes them out with him. A phone begins to ring in the background.

ACT THREE

Scene One

Lights rise on an empty bathroom.

The taps dripping.

DAVID (*from off*). Marian… Marian…

    Lights fall.

Scene Two

Lights rise.

DAVID (*from off*). Marian… Marian…

    DAVID *enters the bathroom.*

    Marian… Marian…

    Beat. He looks around.

    His phone rings. He looks at it.

    Beat. He answers it.

    Hi. Did you get the brochure?… Yeah, we're really excited – we're trying to… You're not?… No… Well, I think if you… No. If it's not right for you… Thanks for letting me know.

    Beat. He disconnects the call. He sits on the floor.

    Beat.

    He looks at his phone.

    He makes a call.

    He waits.

His face drops.

You know I hate answerphones. Where are you?

He disconnects.

He looks around the room. He stands – not sure what to do.

Beat. Lights down.

Scene Three

MARIAN *sits on the floor by the toilet and speaks in the softest voice.*

MARIAN. Because I'm okay, Mum…

I'm actually okay so…

No, I don't want you to come over…

No, I don't want you to come over…

Because I'm okay…

Yes, I am…

Mum, please, I didn't call you so you'd be all fucking pugilistic about it…

Puglisitic…

It's a word…

I like being 'flowery'…

Then just…

Is that the important thing right now…?

Mum…

It's just today…

It's late…

Yeah.

MARIAN *disconnects.*

She sits for an age.

Then she puts on her headphones.

Vous l'avez en magasin?

Vous l'avez en magasin?

Beat. She stands, she stretches, she creaks, she takes some face cream out of the cupboard and begins to apply it.

Quel est votre dernier prix?

Quel est votre dernier prix?

Beat.

Vous me faites un prix d'ami?

Vous me faites un prix d'ami?

DAVID *enters the bathroom. He's carrying a glass with whisky in it.*

MARIAN *turns off the iPod and takes off the headphones.*

They stand there for a moment.

Pause.

DAVID. I've called Paul.

Beat.

MARIAN. Right.

DAVID. I've told him I'm not coming in tomorrow…

Beat.

MARIAN. Right.

Pause.

DAVID. I thought we could take a trip.

And I'm sort of…

The main problem is we're trying to sell something no one wants. We're pretty good at selling it. But that's our main problem.

Pause.

I mean, it's mainly you, my – main – sole really reason for taking the day is – you.

I thought we could take a trip.

MARIAN. Right. Where?

Pause.

DAVID. To – a forest or a beach or something...

MARIAN. Right. Okay.

DAVID. Or a – we could go walking or just – eat somewhere and... Or just do something. We could even go to a cinema. I don't know the last time was when I saw a film during the day. I imagine it'll feel quite – odd.

Do you want that? A trip, I mean, not – the cinema – necessarily...

MARIAN. Yeah. Maybe.

DAVID. I'm sorry.

Beat. His face breaks as if it's about to cry and then he controls himself.

I feel like I've cut my arm off or something.

I feel like I should cut my arm off or something.

I'm really sorry.

MARIAN. I know.

Beat.

DAVID. Sometimes I sit in a room and I just feel...

Today I sat in a room – surrounded by people and it just looked like they were all – talking.

You know how sometimes it can look like everyone is talking all at once.

How everyone is talking all the time. And you're just – trying to –

Sometimes I sit in a room and I feel like I'm not in a room.

It's funny isn't it – missing something – missing something when you're not sure what the thing would now – be.

I don't know.

It's not about me.

I love you.

MARIAN. Okay.

DAVID. I do.

MARIAN. I know.

DAVID. You're so beautiful.

You make me feel lucky. But, uh...

You're so beautiful.

Beat.

MARIAN. Thanks.

DAVID. But it's always been too important to me that you're beautiful.

Sometimes I look at you and you don't look the way I hoped. Sometimes I look at you and you do.

MARIAN. I think that's normal.

DAVID. But it shouldn't matter so much.

MARIAN. No. That's true.

DAVID. I don't really know what I'm saying...

Do you love me?

MARIAN. Yes.

DAVID. You do?

MARIAN. If you ask a question, David, and I answer it, there's no need to reassure yourself of the – answer.

Pause.

DAVID. Where did you... Where have you been?

Beat.

MARIAN. I went for a walk.

Beat.

DAVID. Yeah?

Beat.

MARIAN. Yes. I heard some kids were setting fire to a car up the rec. So I thought I'd...

DAVID. I heard you talking.

MARIAN. My French tape.

DAVID. I've never totally understood your French tape...

I mean, I support you, in it, extending the brain and... but...

MARIAN. Because it's where I want – old people have a good time over there – it's where I want to die.

DAVID. You want to die in France?

MARIAN. Have I not said before...?

DAVID. No.

MARIAN. But we're not good at remembering, so I could have and...

DAVID. True.

MARIAN. Just to clarify, when you say you're sorry –

DAVID. Very.

MARIAN. Just to clarify – for which bit – are you sorry?

Pause. DAVID *considers.*

You can go in – to work tomorrow. You should go in to work tomorrow. Work will require you tomorrow.

You have figures. You have information to...

DAVID. All of it. I'm sorry for all of it.

MARIAN. That's a shit answer. Specifically – for which bit of today –

DAVID. I don't know which bit.

MARIAN. Okay. You don't? That's – strange.

DAVID. No, I just – for all of it...

MARIAN. Did you want to kill me? Are you sorry for that?
Sorry that you didn't?

DAVID. No. I didn't want to kill you.

MARIAN. Then what did you want?

DAVID. I wanted you to stop.

I think.

I don't know.

MARIAN. I wasn't talking.

DAVID. I wanted you to stop being there.

Yeah. I wanted you to stop.

You used to say it was something good about us – that there
were things we forgot. Like what we did last week. We only
knew – you used to say – we only knew that there were...
that good things happened last night. You said you'd forget
our anniversary if you didn't have an alert on your phone.

MARIAN. I know.

But things have become easier to remember.

Pause.

Sometimes. I used to have a dream –

DAVID. Not another dream...

MARIAN. All the time that was about you cutting open –
cutting me open, taking a pair of scissors and putting one
half inside my vagina –

DAVID. I hate your dreams...

MARIAN. And cutting me open – from there on up. Big
scissors. Dress-making scissors.

I have that dream all the time.

More than the masturbating grass people. I have that one all
the time. Never told you about that.

Never told you about that or my desire to die in France.

Where old people are – old people have a good time in France.

Boules and cards and coffee and weather and…

Pause. DAVID opens his mouth to speak. And then closes it again. A tear drips from one of their faces.

When she… When you… When she… You just had a fucking – look – on your – when she – you had this look on your – face. And that look… that fucking look…

DAVID. I can't stop how my face works.

MARIAN. Of course you can. You don't think I don't…? You don't think my face doesn't…

DAVID. I can't.

I'm not as clever as you. I can't.

MARIAN. You looked like you wanted to spit at me. For being so fucking – defective.

DAVID. Did I?

MARIAN. Football team? You missed a game? You missed a game for your football team?

DAVID. It was – I was being metaphorical.

MARIAN. Were you?

DAVID. No. Yes. I don't know. I was being historical. I don't know. I'm not as clever as you. Well educated. I don't know.

Pause. MARIAN sits on the bath. DAVID thinks, and then sits beside her.

I didn't go to the grave today…

MARIAN. No…

DAVID. I didn't go to the grave today.

MARIAN. No. Don't finish that thought. No excuses.

DAVID. You never listen to me.

MARIAN. Yes. I do actually. I do listen. All the time.

Pause.

You wanted me to stop?

Sometimes I want me to stop too.

And sometimes I want you to stop.

DAVID. I know.

Pause.

MARIAN. The worst thing is… I think – I liked – you – hurting me.

DAVID *looks up and says nothing.* MARIAN *says nothing. The words settle.*

I'm not sure though.

DAVID. Yeah?

Pause.

MARIAN. And that. And that. Don't know what that all means. Catch me next week, folks, to – find – out.

Pause. She can't look at him. He can't look at her.

And you may think my dreams are bad or boring – but you – you grind your teeth and shake in the night so whatever you're… Whatever's going on in that head of yours… Probably it's just about football games.

I'm sorry you missed your football game.

Pause. She turns slowly to look at him. He tries to look back.

Anyway. Anyway. So we need a… So do we… Should we? Can we try it again some time? You hurting me? Can we try that again?

DAVID. What?

MARIAN. I think we should try that thing again.

You hurting me again.

DAVID. What? N…

MARIAN. It's better for you and like I say, I think I like it too.

DAVID. No. I don't…

MARIAN. That way we can both – stop.

DAVID. No…

MARIAN. And actually it made today easier because it stopped the clock in my brain and – for a moment I hated you more than I missed her.

DAVID. I miss – her – too.

MARIAN. So can we try it again? Some time.

Can we try you hurting me again some time? Can we try that? You liked it too, right?

DAVID *looks at her.*

Pause. She doesn't look back.

DAVID. Marian…

Pause. She still doesn't look back.

Marian…

Pause. She still doesn't look back.

Marian…

She looks up at him. They look at each other for too long. He stands and moves away from her. He touches the floor. He doesn't know why. He frowns.

We're going to be okay, you and me, we're going to be okay.

MARIAN. Why?

Pause.

DAVID. Because I can make things right again.

MARIAN. You…

DAVID. I want to be. I think we should be. I just want to be hopeful.

MARIAN. No. You want to be forgetful.

DAVID. No.

MARIAN. Sometimes – don't you think – there was a chance – and we missed it?

DAVID. Yeah. So we now – now we need to make a new chance...

MARIAN. Not make...

DAVID. No. No. I don't mean... I just mean we need to... Try harder to be... Try harder.

MARIAN. Why?

DAVID. Because what else are we going to do.

Pause. MARIAN *considers.*

I'm sorry I tried to... I'm sorry I hurt you. I'm really sorry. And I won't do it again. And I'm – I don't know. And if I do – if I do – I'll kill myself.

MARIAN. Sales pitch.

DAVID. Truth.

Pause. MARIAN *considers.*

MARIAN. Okay.

DAVID. We're going to take a day trip tomorrow. Fuck Paul. Fuck work. Go back to somewhere we remember. Some nice – place.

MARIAN. Okay.

DAVID. Go to that pub in Richmond that does the roasts on the big plates... Go to the park, look at the deer, go to the pub...

MARIAN. Okay. It's not Sunday tomorrow...

DAVID. No. Good point.

MARIAN. So a roast would be...

DAVID. Yeah.

MARIAN. I mean, they probably only get the plates out on...

DAVID. Sunday. Yeah.

Pause. MARIAN *looks up.*

MARIAN. And I'd rather go somewhere new.

DAVID. Okay.

MARIAN. I'd rather go to somewhere new.

Pause.

DAVID. Yes. New is better.

Pause.

Maybe we should go to the cinema…

Maybe we should go to France…

Pause. MARIAN *smiles.*

MARIAN. Maybe we should.

DAVID. And play cards and bowls.

MARIAN. Boules.

DAVID. Bowls.

Pause.

She smiles.

MARIAN. Bowls.

Pause. He sits beside her on the edge of the bath.

DAVID. And if that doesn't work we'll just… hope that…

MARIAN. Yeah.

MARIAN smiles, DAVID smiles, and then they don't.

DAVID. Are you hungry?

I haven't eaten.

Are you hungry?

Talk of the roast has made me… I could fix us some – I can fix us something…

Eggs or noodles or…

We've got those Linda McCartney frozen lasagnes in that your mum said…

They're not too bad.

Pause.

She looks carefully at his face.

MARIAN. Yeah. I think…

Maybe…

We deserve each other.

DAVID. Do we?

MARIAN. Information gatherers. Information deleterers. Information… what's the opposite of information? Misinformation?

DAVID. Ignorance?

Pause. MARIAN *considers this. She looks at her hands and then up at him.*

MARIAN. You'll hurt me again. Just so you know. You will.

And I'll probably be quite forgiving. Again.

Because we deserve each other.

Beat. DAVID *looks at her. And says nothing.*

Yeah, I can be fed – I'm hungry…

And actually – I'd quite like to get drunk.

ACT FOUR

Scene One

DAVID *comes in.*

He looks around, he's drunk.

He looks at the mirror.

He does a James Bond-style gun-move at the mirror.

DAVID. I'm fucking...

He does a little dance move.

He undoes his trousers.

He begins to piss. He doesn't pull the seat up.

He can't piss.

He tries hard. He pisses a little. It goes all over the seat.

He starts to sing. He stops pissing. He looks at himself, annoyed. He tears off some toilet paper, dick still out and rudimentally cleans the seat. He dumps the paper in the bowl. He laughs. He sings a few lines of the Record Breakers' *theme tune.*

He puts up the seat. He puts his foot on the toilet rim. He tries to piss some more.

He does piss. He laughs.

A phone begins to ring offstage. He looks towards it. Distracted.

The lights slowly fade.

A Nick Hern Book

Mydidae first published in Great Britain as a paperback original in 2012 by Nick Hern Books Limited, The Glasshouse, 49a Goldhawk Road, London W12 8QP, in association with DryWrite and Soho Theatre

Mydidae copyright © 2012 Jack Thorne

Jack Thorne has asserted his right to be identified as the author of this work

Cover image: Lucy Patrick Ward
Cover design: Ned Hoste, 2H

Typeset by Nick Hern Books
Printed in Great Britain by Mimeo Ltd, St Ives, Cambs, PE27 3LE

A CIP catalogue record for this book is available from the British Library

ISBN   978 1 84842 315 2